Presented to

....

From

....

On this date

....

❧

THINKING of YOU

ELLYN SANNA

A DayMaker Greeting Book

OUT *of*

THE *Abundance*

OF THE *Heart*

the mouth speaks.

MATTHEW 12.34 KJV

WHENEVER

I think

I remember the laughter we've shared

I recall the burdens you've lightened

I rejoice at the way our relationship continues to grow

And I thank God for the way you've shown me His love

of *You*

I thank my God

every time

I remember you.

PHILIPPIANS 1:3

God gave us Memories that we might have roses in December

JAMES M. BARRIE

LAUGHTER
SHARED

———◦———

❧

WHEN I THINK of YOU

(I ALWAYS SMILE)

I remember the silly adventures we've had together...
the embarrassing moments that sent us into giggles...the
magic moments when all we could do was laugh out
loud...the long talks that were always sprinkled with
laughter. You and I have had so many reasons to laugh
together. The funny things just seem funnier when we're
together (you help me find the laughter that's hidden
even in my darkest days). I'm grateful for all the laughs
we've shared.

Laughter is the sun

that drives winter

from the human face.

VICTOR HUGO

Laughter O, glorious laughter! thou man-loving spirit, that for a time doth take the burden from the weary back, that doth lay salve to the weary feet, bruised and cut by flints and shards.

DOUGLAS JERROLD

To every thing there is a season, and a time to every purpose under the heaven: A time to weep, and a time laugh.   ECCLESIASTES 3:1,4 KJV

Salt is like good humor, and nearly every thing is better for a pinch of it.   LOUISA MAY ALCOTT

Laughter is the closest thing to the grace of God.

KARL BARTH

The most wasted of all days is one without laughter.

E. E. CUMMINGS

To have joy one must share it—
happiness was born a twin.
LORD BYRON

One can never speak enough of the virtues. . .
the power of shared laughter.
FRANCOISE SAGA

Among those whom I like,
I can find no common denominator,
But among those whom I love, I can:
All of them make me laugh.
W. H. AUDEN

One can bear grief, but it takes two to be glad.
ELBERT HUBBARD

Our mouths
were filled
with laughter,
our tongues
with songs of joy.

Laughter is the shortest distance
between two people.
VICTOR BORGE

"Blessed are you who weep now,
for you will laugh."
LUKE 6:21

"[God] will yet fill your mouth with
laughter and your lips with shouts of joy."
JOB 8:21

From quiet homes and first beginning,
Out to the undiscovered ends,
There's nothing worth the wear of winning,
But laughter and the love of friends.
HILLAIRE BELLOC

I have known sorrow—therefore I may laugh with you,
O friend, more merrily than those who never sorrowed
upon earth. And know not laughter's worth. I have
known laughter—therefore I may sorrow with you far
more tenderly than those who never guess how sad a
thing seems merriment to one heart's suffering.

THEODOSIA GARRISON

Friendship that flows from the heart cannot be frozen
by adversity, as the water that flows from the spring
cannot congeal in winter.

JAMES FENIMORE COOPER

Of all the things God created, I am often most
grateful He created laughter.

CHARLES SWINDOLL

BURDENS
LIGHTENED

Carry ecah other's

burdens and in this way you

will fulfill the law of Christ.

GALATIANS 6:2

✤

WHEN I THINK of YOU

(I REMEMBER YOU HELD ME UP)

Some days I just can't see anything funny about my life. When talking with you, though, I begin to see from a new perspective. I stop taking life so seriously— and before I know it, I begin to laugh. After sharing time with you, I return to my life with a fresh outlook. The world's not ending after all—God's love and joy still surround me. Thanks for sharing your laughter with me.

Friendship is a strong and habitual inclination
in two persons to promote the good and happiness
of one another   EUSTACE BUDGELL

You have been a creative force in my life.

Where I have experienced pain,
you helped me find healing.

Where I have felt weakness,
you have showed me strength.

Where I have experienced loss,
you have helped me find renewed faith.

Your creative approach to life
has changed mine for today,

for always.

VIOLA RUELKE GOMMER

My friends have made the story of my
life. In a thousand ways they have turned
my limitations into beautiful privileges
and enabled me to walk serene and happy
in the shadow cast by my deprivation.

HELEN KELLER

The most I can do for my friend
is simply to be his friend.
I have no wealth to bestow on him.
If he knows that I am happy in loving him,
he will want no other reward.
Is not friendship divine in this?

HENRY DAVID THOREAU

Rejoice with
them that do
rejoice, and
weep with them
that weep.

ROMANS 12:15 KJV

Pray for my soul.
More things are wrought by prayer
Than this world dreams of.
ALFRED LORD TENNYSON

Two people can accomplish more than twice as much as one: they get a better return for their labor. If one person falls, the other can reach out and help. But people who are alone when they fall are in real trouble. And on a cold night, two under the same blanket can gain warmth from each other. But how can one be warm alone? A person standing alone can be attacked and defeated, but two can stand back-to-back and conquer.
ECCLESIASTES 4:9–12 NLT

Therefore encourage one another and build
each other up, just as in fact you are doing.
1 THESSALONIANS 5:11

"Trouble shared is trouble halved."
DOROTHY SAYERS

A true friend is one who is there
when you fall apart and is still there
to help you pick up the pieces and hold
you while you put yourself back together.
LORI SHANKLE

Holy friendship that has medicine
for all the wretchedness is not
to be despised. From God it truly is,
that amid the wretchedness of exile,
we be comforted with the counsel of
friends until we come to Him.
RICHARD ROLLE

SOMETIMES IN LIFE, YOU FIND A SPECIAL FRIEND. Someone who changes your life just by being a part of it. Someone who makes you laugh until you can't stop. Someone who makes you believe that there really is good in the world. Someone who convinces you that there really is an unlocked door just waiting for you to open it. This is forever friendship.

When you're down and the world seems dark and empty, your forever friend lifts you up in spirit and makes that dark and empty world suddenly seem bright and full. Your forever friend gets you through the hard times, the sad times, and the confused times. If you turn and walk away, your forever friend follows. If you lose your way, your forever friend guides you. Your forever friend holds your hand and assures you everything is going to be okay. If you find such a friend, you feel happy and complete because you need not worry. You have a forever friend, and forever has no end. AUTHOR UNKNOWN

At times my life seems bitter to the taste.

At times my cup of life seems empty.

We share who we are in conversation,

As we speak of life, its gains and losses.

And my cup is refilled:

The taste of bitterness turns sweet.

A cheerful heart is good medicine.

PROVERBS 17:22

Thank you for always sticking with me!
Please know you can always count on me
to be there when you need me.

Thus nature has no love for solitude, and always
leans, as it were, on some support, and the sweetest
support is found in the most intimate friendship.

CICERO

No soul is desolate as long as there is a human
being for whom it can feel trust and reverence.
GEORGE ELIOT

There are "friends" who destroy each other,
but a real friend sticks closer than a brother.
PROVERBS 18:24 NLT

Trouble is the sieve through which we sift our
acquaintances. Those too big to pass through are
our friends.
ARLENE FRANCIS

I thank my God always on your behalf.
1 CORINTHIANS 1:4 KJV

GROWING
CLOSER

———⊱◈⊰———

Night and day

I constantly remember

you in my prayers.

2 TIMOTHY 1:3 NIV

WHEN I THINK of YOU

(I APPRECIATE YOU MORE)

As the years have passed, our relationship has changed and grown, but we will never outgrow one another.

Thank you for accepting the ways I've changed over the years. I rely on your genuine understanding of who I am in my heart, despite the outer changes. In this world that whirls so quickly 'round me, I count on you as one of the stable constants in my life, one I can always count on no matter what. Time will bring new experiences for each of us. Please know my love for you will never change. I look forward to growing even closer.

The
best mirror
is an old
friend.

GEORGE
HERBERT

Sometimes our light goes out but is blown into flame
by another human being Each of us owes deepest
thanks to those who have rekindled this light.

ALBERT SCHWEITZER

You are such a special friend to me. When we are
apart, you are constantly in my thoughts, my prayers,
my heart. No matter how long it has been, time
disappears when we are back together.

LORI SHANKLE

Time shared with you is precious.
No need to explain.
You seem to hear my thoughts.
No words need be spoken.
Time shared with you is precious.
Peace and joy fill my heart once more.

VIOLA RUELKE GOMMER

I awoke this morning with devout thanksgiving
for my friends, the old and the new.
Shall I not call God, the Beautiful, who daily
showeth Himself to me in His gifts.
RALPH WALDO EMERSON

If you have any encouragement from being united with
Christ, if any comfort from his love, if any fellowship
with the Spirit, if any tenderness and compassion, then
make my joy complete by being like-minded, having the
same love, being one in spirit and purpose.

Each of you should look not only to your own
interests, but also to the interests of others. Your attitude
should be the same as that of Christ Jesus.
PHILIPPIANS 2:1-2, 4-5

You are good medicine.
VIOLA RUELKE GOMMER

Two may talk together under the same roof for many
years, yet never really meet; and two others at first
speech are old friends.

MARY CATHERWOOD

One day held the memory of you. . .
And sowed the sky with tiny clouds of love.

ROBERT BROOKE

Hand grasps hand,
eye lights eye. . .
And great hearts expand,
And grow. . . .

ROBERT BROWNING

Do you know that conversation
is one of the greatest pleasures in life?

SOMERSET MAUGHAM

But, after all, the very best thing in talk,
and the thing that helps the most, is
friendship. How it dissolves the barriers
that divide us and loosens all constraint
and diffuses itself like some fine old cordial
through all the veins of life—this feeling
that we understand and trust each other
and wish each other heartily well! Everything into which it really comes is good.

HENRY VAN DYKE

I count myself in nothing else so happy
As in a soul rememb'ring my good friends.

WILLIAM SHAKESPEARE

Friends have all things in common.

PLATO

A friend may well be reckoned the masterpiece of nature.

RALPH WALDO EMERSON

When I say, thank you for your smile,
You say, pass it on.
When I say, thank you for your listening ear,
You say, do the same for another.
When I say, thank you for your encouragement,
You say, offer the same to someone else.
When I say, thank you for keeping my secret,
You say, do the same for someone else.
Your simple example and quiet wisdom
Have taught me generosity of spirit.
Thank you. I will follow your lead.

VIOLA RUELKE GOMMER

One can never pay in gratitude;
one can only pay "in kind" somewhere else in life.
ANNE MORROW LINDBERGH

"Do to others as you would have them do to you."
LUKE 6:31

The heartfelt counsel of a friend is as sweet
as perfume and incense. As iron sharpens iron,
a friend sharpens a friend.
PROVERBS 27:9, 17 NLT

Gratitude is one of those things that cannot be bought.
LORD HALIFAX

I cannot but remember such things were,
That were most precious to me.
WILLIAM SHAKESPEARE

I CANNOT IMAGINE MY LIFE WITHOUT YOU. You are the one I call when I'm delighted and proud—and you're the one I want to talk with when I'm crying. I depend on you to understand my thoughts and feelings. I know on my hardest days I can rely on your prayers supporting me all the way. I could get by with less money and fewer possessions—but I wouldn't want to get along without you. You are truly one of my life's greatest treasures.

Our friendship through the years has made our patchwork lives into a lovely tapestry. The threads woven through simple pieces of fabric are respect, affection, appreciation, admiration, support, comfort, forgiveness, patience, refuge, joy, and laughter. These priceless threads of gold and silver strengthen and beautify the texture of our friendship. Each year the tapestry of our relationship grows more valuable.

VIOLA RUELKE GOMMER

ALWAYS
LOVING

———◦◦◦———

To see your face

is like seeing the

face of God.

GENESIS 33:10

WHEN I THINK of YOU

(I GIVE THANKS TO GOD)

I realize how much I have learned from you. You have shared your insights with me, your wisdom, your understanding. You have taught me so much. Most of all, you have helped me to see God's face.

So many times God used your hands to touch my life, your words to speak comfort to my soul, and your heart to bring me His love.

I guess that's why whenever I think of you, I thank God!

Some people come into our lives and quickly go.
Some stay for awhile and leave footprints on our
hearts. And we are never, ever the same.
AUTHOR UNKNOWN

Never shall I forget the days
which I spent with you.
LUDWIG VAN BEETHOVEN

It is very easy to forgive others their mistakes,
it takes more grit and gumption
to forgive them for having witnessed our own.
JESSAMYN WEST

A friend is a gift you give yourself.
ROBERT LOUIS STEVENSON

You are

welcome

as flowers

in May.

WILLIAM
SHAKESPEARE

It suddenly seemed to me that we had always been near each other and that we would always be so. . . .

It was one of those tender and peaceful feelings which are like a gift flowing from a region higher than ourselves, illuminating the future and deepening the present. From that moment our understanding was perfect. . . .
RAISSA MARTIAIN

Words satisfy the soul as food satisfies
the stomach, the right words on a
person's lips bring satisfaction.
PROVERBS 18:20 NLT

Thank you for all the times you've said exactly the right thing to me! I pray our relationship will continue to grow. I see God's love through you.

"Stay" is a charming word
in a friend's vocabulary.
LOUISA MAY ALCOTT

You have seen me at my worst—
and yet somehow, it never matters.
If anything, we just keep growing closer
the more painfully honest
we are with each other.
Thank you for putting up with me!

Only friends will tell you the truths
you need to hear to make. . . .
your life bearable.
FRANCINE
DU PLESSIX GRAY

We always thank God for. . .you, mentioning
you in our prayers. 1 THESSALONIANS 1:2

How different we are!
You are tall, thin, fair,
and always on time.
I am shorter, wider, darker,
and usually late.
What makes us friends?
What makes us friends
are what we cherish—
Family, friends, and faith.
We may be different,
But we are soul close.
VIOLA RUELKE GOMMER

Every true friend is a glimpse of God.
LUCY LARCOM

I have learned that to have a good friend
is the purest of all God's gifts. . . .
FRANCES FARMER

No one has ever seen God, but if we love one
another, God lives in us and his love is made
complete in us.
1 JOHN 4:12

Love is a flower that grows in any soil, works its
sweet miracles undaunted by autumn frost or winter
snow, blooming fair and fragrant all the year, and
blessing those who give and those who receive.
LOUISA MAY ALCOTT

The best and most beautiful things in the world
cannot be seen or even touched. They must be felt
with the heart.
HELEN KELLER

I owe

thee much . . . .

Far, far

beyond what

I can ever pay.

ROBERT BLAIR

Thank You

(YOU ARE A TREASURE)

You listen patiently when I'm hurting. You cry with me, and help me to laugh again. You are often more proud of me than I am of myself.

With no thought of reward, you give of yourself— you walk with me, you show me God.

Thinking of You—Deluxe DayMaker

© 2002 by Barbour Publishing, Inc.

ISBN 1-58660-708-1

Cover art © PhotoDisc., Inc.

All Scripture quotations, unless otherwise indicated, are taken from the HOLY BIBLE, NEW
INTERNATIONAL VERSION®, NIV®. Copyright © 1973, 1978, 1984 by International Bible Society.
Used by permission of Zondervan Publishing House. All rights reserved.

Scripture quotations marked KJV are taken from the King James Version of the Bible.

Scripture quotations marked NLT are taken from the *Holy Bible*, New Living Translation,
copyright ©1996. Used by permission of Tyndale House Publishers, Inc.
Wheaton, Illinois 60189, U.S.A. All rights reserved.

Selections by Viola Ruelke Gommer are used with the author's permission.

Published by Barbour Books, an imprint of Barbour Publishing, Inc.,
P.O. Box 719, Uhrichsville, Ohio 44683, www.barbourbooks.com

Member of the
Evangelical Christian
Publishers Association

Printed in China.

5 4 3 2 1